The Erie: The History and Legacy of the Native American Group

By Charles River Editors

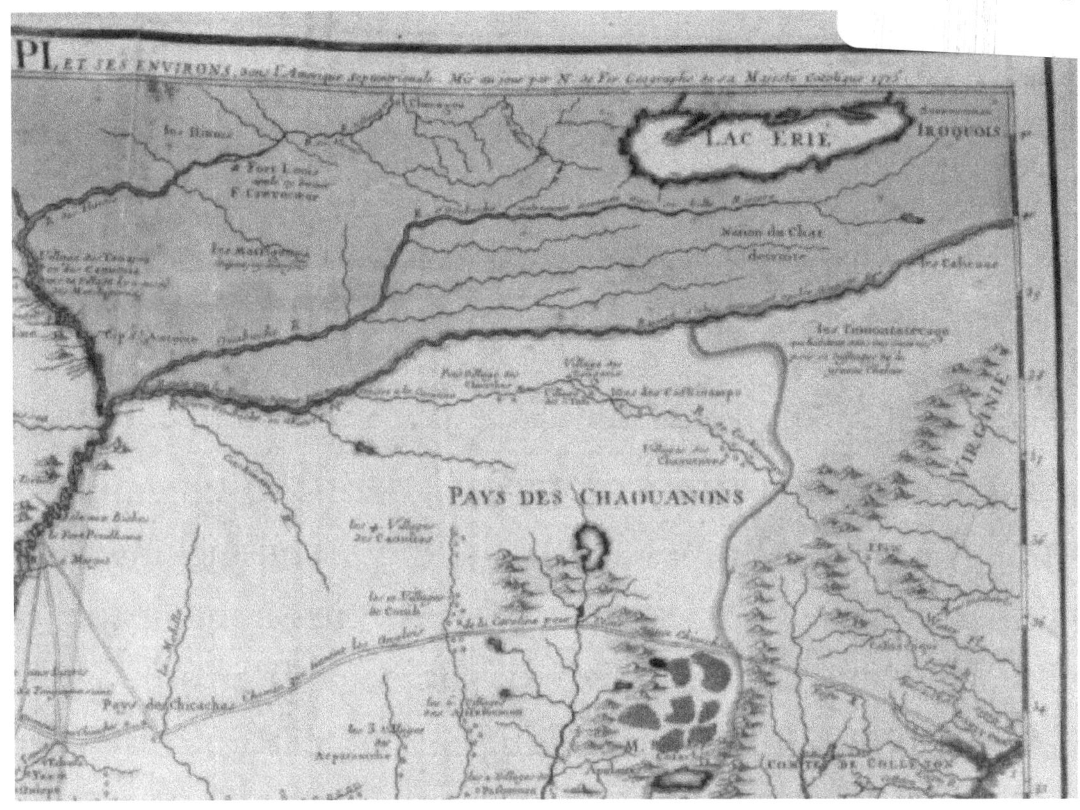

A 1715 map of the region

About Charles River Editors

Charles River Editors provides superior editing and original writing services across the digital publishing industry, with the expertise to create digital content for publishers across a vast range of subject matter. In addition to providing original digital content for third party publishers, we also republish civilization's greatest literary works, bringing them to new generations of readers via ebooks.

Sign up here to receive updates about free books as we publish them, and visit Our Kindle Author Page to browse today's free promotions and our most recently published Kindle titles.

Introduction

Along the sandy shores and ancient forests of crystal blue Lake Erie, a proud, brave, and confident people lived long ago, building homes, raising crops, hunting game, rearing children, and surviving through harsh winters and hot summers. None of their tribe remains today to tell their story, but their name lives on in the waters of a Great Lake. The Erie Tribe would have been completely lost to history if not for the archeological evidence and archival records that have been uncovered to prove that they existed. The Erie was a relatively small nation; at its height, their population numbered about ten thousand. Archeologist Frederick Houghton writes that archeological evidence proves that Erie culture coincided in "nearly every aspect" with other Iroquoian tribes of the eastern Great Lakes area, which means that historians, anthropologists, and archeologists can understand a great deal about the Erie by studying their cousins, the Iroquois, with whom they also shared a language.

Among all the Native American tribes, the Iroquois people are some of the most well documented Native Americans in history. Indigenous to the northeast region of what is now the United States and parts of Canada, they were among some of the earliest contacts Europeans had with the native tribes. And yet they have remained a constant source of mystery. The name "Iroquois", like many Native American tribal names, is not a name the people knew themselves by, but a word applied to them by their enemies the Huron, who called them "Iroquo" (rattlesnake) as an insult. The French later added the suffix "ois." Moreover, the Iroquois are not even a single tribe but a confederation of several different tribal nations that include the Seneca, Oneida, Onondaga, Mohawk, Cayuga and the Tuscarora, who didn't become part of the union until the early 1700's. The name Haudenosaunee (pronounced "ho-den-oh-SHO-nee") is the name the people use for themselves, which translates as "the People of the Longhouse." They are also commonly known as the Six Nations.

Despite their own cultural differences, the nations that comprised the Iroquois Confederacy established their political dominance across much of America's East Coast and Midwest through conquest, and it is that aspect which has perhaps best endured among Americans in terms of the Iroquois' legacy. European settlers who came into contact with the Mohawks in the Northeast certainly learned to respect their combat skills, to the point that there were literally bounties on the Mohawks' heads, with scalps fetching money for colonists who succeeded in slaying them and carrying away the "battle prize".

As it turned out, the Erie would experience some of the Iroquois' martial abilities the hard way, because in the mid-17th century, a bitter civil war erupted among the various tribes of the Iroquois Nation which would prove disastrous for the Erie, virtually wiping them out of existence. Luckily, historians have discovered many remains of this vanquished people in mounds, graves, and village sites, revealing a great deal about how they lived, worked, and died. By analyzing these abundant archeological clues, scholars have been able to solve many mysteries about these intelligent, resourceful, and artistic people.

The Erie's Origins

The Erie people belong to a group of Native American tribes known as the Iroquois Nation, all of whom have a common ancestry and anthropological record and can trace their origins back to the first humans who ever settled in North America during the most recent Ice Age. Ancient *Homo sapiens* traveled over the Bering Strait from Siberia to Alaska at least 35,000 years ago in search of food, a better climate, or natural resources. Over the next 20,000 years, humans would be dispersed throughout the entire Western Hemisphere. These early Americans traveled in small family groups or clans, and simply called themselves, "the people." Skeletal remains show that these Paleo-Indians lived with early horses, bison, camels, mammoth, and mastodon, which they hunted for food in addition to scavenging for plants.

According to historian Harry Forrest Lupold, these archaic people and their descendants used 275 species of plants for medicine, 130 for food, 27 for smoking, 25 as dyes, and 18 in beverages.[1] Over time, unique local cultures emerged in the form of tribes who developed customs and practices depending on the land on which they lived. Those who lived in the forests of present-day Canada would develop very different ways of life than

---

[1] Lupold, Harry Forrest, The Forgotten People: The Woodland Erie, (Hicksville, New York: Exposition Press, 1975), page 5.

those who settled in the deserts of Mexico or the coastal lands of Brazil.

The Wisconsin Ice Sheet covered the Great Lakes until about 11000 BCEE, and man arrived in the area for the first time soon afterward.[2] Remnants of glaciers remained in the valleys of prehistoric mountains, creating the Great Lakes. The woodland people who settled in this area of North America lived in small groups in the forests, hunting game, fishing, and gathering nuts, acorns, roots, and berries. Historians know little about their daily life, except that they used bone, shell and copper for tools. The great majority of their time was spent searching for food, so there was little opportunity for casual pursuits like pottery, jewelry-making, or even warfare. Their main hunting weapon was spear-like, and they lived nomadic lives in movable camps.[3]

The Iroquois peoples, including the Erie, descended from two groups of early North American peoples known as the Adena and the Hopewell cultures. Around the sixth century CE, the woodland people described above migrated south of the Ohio River into present-day Kentucky, West Virginia, Indiana, and Pennsylvania.[4] Archeologists have dubbed this group the Adena culture and people of this group lived in small settlements near

---

[2] Lupold, The Forgotten People: The Woodland Erie, 8.
[3] Lupold, The Forgotten People: The Woodland Erie, 5.
[4] Lupold, The Forgotten People: The Woodland Erie, 6.

the abundant streams and rivers in this verdant area. Around their settlements, they usually built earthen walls that stood about five feet tall and inside these walls, people lived in round houses built of saplings with central posts and bark-covered roofs. They raised corn in addition to hunting, fishing, and gathering. They made crude pottery, and they used copper, mica, and stone to manufacture other tools and supplies.

In the 1920s, archeologists uncovered remnants of a different Native American society at the Hopewell Farm in Ross County, Ohio, thus these people became known as the Hopewell culture. They were an amalgamation of Adenas and other peoples. It was later determined that a common Hopewell culture extended from New York to Louisiana and west to Kansas. The Hopewell group is known as the most prominent society of people to inhabit the present-day United States before Columbus arrived in 1492.[5] Later native tribes, including the Iroquois and Erie, were their descendants.

The Hopewell were known as the "Mound Builders" because they built large geometric earth mounds for protection as well as burial sites, some of which can still be visited today in Ohio. Skilled architects, the Hopewell built large systems of earthen walls as well as mounds for religious ceremonies and funerals. Tomb offerings were

[5] Lupold, The Forgotten People: The Woodland Erie, 7.

commonly found inside burial mounds, suggesting a hierarchical system within the community, where those in higher social or political positions were often buried with valuable possessions, such as sculptures, furs, and ornaments. Their artistic sculptures were legendary, with expertly set pearls, shells and copper as well as cut and carved mica, stone, and bone. Archeologists have also uncovered elaborately carved clay and stone tobacco pipes featuring animal and bird motifs.[6]

A picture of the Grave Creek Mound in present-day Moundsville, West Virginia

Hopewell settlements, built along rivers and streams, were generally small and temporary. They resided in one area for a time and then relocated to find fresh resources

---

[6] Lupold, The Forgotten People: The Woodland Erie, 7.

or better trade routes. Their homes were rectangular with thatched roofs and dried mud walls. The Hopewell were the first Native American culture to develop reliable agricultural skills, growing sunflowers, squash, and maygrass. As they improved on their methods through the generations, agriculture eclipsed hunting as the primary means of sustenance.

For reasons unknown, the Hopewell Culture started to decline around the fifth century CE. This is probably a result of warfare with other cultures, which increased following the introduction of the bow and arrow.[7] Hopewell societies may have become more secluded for protection from enemies, or members assimilated into other more dominant groups. As the fur trade began to take up more time and effort, mound building declined,[8] and, over generations, the Hopewell and Adena cultures morphed into other Native American nations, including the Algonquians, Iroquois, and Sioux.

The Iroquois and the Algonquian cultures, descendants of the Adenas and Hopewells, began to emerge in the present-day American Midwest late in the Mound Building era. The Iroquois built smaller earth mounds than the Hopewells, usually over the dead as a way to

---

[7] "Hopewell Culture," Hopewell Culture - Ohio History Central, accessed August 22, 2020, https://ohiohistorycentral.org/w/Hopewell_Culture.
[8] Vietzen, Raymond Charles, Indians of the Lake Erie Basin, or Lost Nations, (Wahoo, Nebraska: Ludi Printing Co., 1865), page 150.

cover their bodies, honor them, and mark the grave for eternity.[9] The Algonquians were the largest group of Adena-Hopewell descendants, scattered throughout the territory from present-day Canada to Virginia. As the Iroquois people migrated westward from 800 to 1600 CE, probably to escape from the Algonquians or to find better trade routes and resources, many new tribes splintered off as they traveled on different geographic courses.[10] As they reached Lake Erie, for example, one group went north of the lake, and one went south. The northern group became known as the Neutral Tribe, while the southern band became the Eries. The Eastern Woodland cultures, as archeologists call them, dominated the eastern half of the present-day United States, from the Atlantic Coast to the prairies, from the St. Lawrence River to the Carolinas. These cultures are known as the Iroquois Nation because they all spoke a common language and had similar customs, but individual tribes existed, including the Erie, Seneca, Mohawk, Huron, Oneida, and several others. All Iroquois groups share four definitive archeological characteristics, however: deep refuse pits containing animal bones and pottery fragments, tools mostly made from bone or antler instead of stone, small, triangular arrow points, and round-bottomed clay pots decorated with a chevron pattern.[11]

---

[9] Vietzen, Indians of the Lake Erie Basin, or Lost Nations, 23.
[10] Lupold, The Forgotten People: The Woodland Erie, 9.
[11] Houghton, Frederick. "The Characteristics of Iroquoian Village Sites of Western New York,"

The Erie were closely related ethnically and geographically to the Seneca tribe although the two tribes were mortal enemies. Archeologist Frederick Houghton, by analyzing dig sites of several Iroquois groups, has determined that "all the characteristics of the Seneca were common also to the Erie branch of Iroquois."[12] The Squawkihows and Kah-Kwahs were smaller branches of the Erie tribe. Little was understood about Native American tribal systems by the Europeans who first recorded their existence. Many different branches, clans, and bands might have been considered part of the same nation or culture although each band lived separately and had its own unique customs and practices, much like various dialects and ethnic cultures have developed within the same geographical borders of nations known today. Therefore, European written records, while helpful, cannot always be relied upon for accuracy.

Unfortunately, the Iroquois had no written language to record their own history, so European writings are all that historians have. The Erie were obliterated in 1653, not long after the first European settlers arrived in their land, so there are only a handful of European records regarding them. Since very few written records of the Erie exist, historians, archeologists, and anthropologists rely mostly

American Anthropologist, vol. 18, no. 4, 1916, JSTOR, www.jstor.org/stable/660120. Accessed 3 August 2020, 297.
[12] Houghton, "The Characteristics of Iroquoian Village Sites of Western New York," 515.

on archeological evidence to understand how this society lived. The Erie, like other Native Americans, did not have a written language, although they sometimes used pictographs. There is virtually no writing from Native Americans themselves, only what European and American explorers and settlers wrote about them. Most of what is known today about the Erie tribe comes from archeological evidence found underground during the construction of farms, homes, businesses, roads, bridges, and other modern structures. One large Erie village, for example, was unearthed during the erection of a steel plant in Lorain County, Ohio in the twentieth century, three hundred years after their demise.

By analyzing the human and animal remains and artifacts found in these locations, anthropologists and archeologists can determine a great deal about the Erie. The many bodies of adolescents and children show that life expectancy was rather short and infant mortality was high; most died before age 35.[13] Lack of adequate shelter and nutrition meant only the hardiest children and teens survived, leading to a small but strong population.[14]

According to skeletal remains, the Erie were slightly taller than most Native Americans: men averaged five feet, ten inches, and women averaged five feet, two

---

[13] Vietzen, Indians of the Lake Erie Basin, or Lost Nations, 157.
[14] Vietzen Indians of the Lake Erie Basin, or Lost Nations, 179.

inches. Archeologists have found some male skeletons as tall as six feet, six inches, leading them to think that Erie warriors were powerful and strong. According to Vietzen, "large men were the rule and not the exception."[15] Skull structure shows that the Erie had long, broad faces and broad noses.[16]

The Erie were named for the huge lake they lived just south of, and they occupied territory in a triangular swath all along the lower coast of Lake Erie southward to present-day Pittsburgh. Their homeland stretched over four hundred miles east-to-west and one hundred miles north-to-south. They built densely-populated villages along the numerous rivers and streams that drained into Lake Erie and fortified their villages with earthen walls or wooden palisades made of logs set vertically in the ground, usually about ten feet high.[17] To ensure that the palisade poles lasted longer, they removed the bark by heating logs over a small fire, then pouring warm water over them, which allowed the bark to be scraped off with chisels made of antler or bone. Sometimes, villages were also surrounded by ditches. Watchtowers and stone stations with signal fires might also stand on the river banks near an Erie village. There were at least 28 such villages and twelve forts at the beginning of the

[15] Vietzen, Indians of the Lake Erie Basin, or Lost Nations, 101.
[16] Vietzen, Indians of the Lake Erie Basin, or Lost Nations, 180.
[17] Lupold, The Forgotten People: The Woodland Erie, 29.

seventeenth century; most were between eight and ten miles apart.[18] Artifacts discovered at each of these has provided archeologists, anthropologists, and historians with valuable information about Erie society. The largest village and Erie capital, Riqué, which meant "place of the panther," was located somewhere between Buffalo, New York and Erie, Pennsylvania.[19]

Living near water, the Eries' primary mode of transport was the canoe, but they also traveled on foot, using snowshoes in the winter. Canoes were built out of elm bark, which was peeled from the trees and pounded into flat splints that could be split and shaved to whatever size they needed.[20] Ribs made of saplings lined the bottom and sides of canoes, and wooden planks were laid in the bottom to sit or stand on. Pitch, a natural tar-like substance, was smeared along the bottom and seams to make the vessel waterproof. One person usually paddled these canoes while standing in the stern, but several people could fit inside. Birchbark canoes were light enough to carry around waterfalls and obstructions, strong enough to transport several tons of gear, furs, or meat, and sturdy enough to last for several years.[21] Bark was used to

---

[18] Dye, David H. "Rotten Palisade Posts and Rickety Baffle Gates: Repairing Native Eastern North American Fortifications." Archaeological Perspectives on Warfare on the Great Plains, edited by Andrew J. Clark and Douglas B. Bamforth, University Press of Colorado, Louisville; Colorado, 2018, JSTOR, www.jstor.org/stable/j.ctvgd21w.7. Accessed 19 Aug. 2020, 145–176.
[19] Lupold, The Forgotten People: The Woodland Erie, 26.
[20] Vietzen, Indians of the Lake Erie Basin, or Last Nations, 150.
[21] Kimm, S.C., The Iroquois: A History of the Six Nations of New York, (Middleburgh, New York: Press of Pierre W. Danforth, 1900), 304.

manufacture a variety of useful objects in addition to canoes and longhouse walls, including barrels, carrying trays, ropes and straps. The bark was boiled in a mixture of ashes and water to make it soft, then dried and separated into filaments which could be braided into rope.

Daily Life

Like other woodland tribes of the Great Lakes area, the Erie lived in rectangular longhouses built of wooden frames covered in sheets of elm bark with entrances at both ends and stone-lined fire pits in the center. Unlike the multi-family homes of most Iroquois tribes, Erie longhouses were smaller, single-family units, about ten feet wide and twenty feet long. Each home had its own fire pit in the center of the house, and time around the family fire, or "mother's circle," was the only period of real relaxation or enjoyment in the Eries' long, arduous day.[22]

Occasionally, more than one family would share a larger house, up to 35 feet long, but each family unit, called an *Ohwachera*, had its own hearth for cooking and eating.[23] To build their homes, the Erie constructed a wooden frame of strong saplings set into the ground and bent together at the tops to form a rounded roof structure. Other poles were bound transversely to the rafters and

[22] Vietzen, Indians of the Lake Erie Basin, or Lost Nations, 26.
[23] Vietzen, Indians of the Lake Erie Basin, or Lost Nations, 162.

along the sides to reinforce the frame. Large sheets of birch, elm, oak, spruce, or white cedar bark covered the roof and walls in the same manner as modern-day shingles to allow water to run off the building when it rained or snowed. Openings were left in the roof for smoke vents. Inside, wide scaffolds were built up off the floor along both sides with bark platforms lined with skins for sleeping. Firewood was stored under these beds to keep it dry. Dried and cured foods, meats, herbs, weapons, and tools hung from the roof poles beyond the reach of wild animals on the ground.

Archeologists have also discovered caves and grottos inhabited by the Erie, including Shelter Cave in Cascade Park in Lorain County, Ohio. This grotto, high in the cliffs on the banks of the Black River, which measures about fifty feet long and fifteen feet wide, was probably a winter home, as it offered protection from rain and snow. Archeologists have found skeletons at least four hundred years old here, as well as arrowheads and potsherds.[24]

A never-ending quest for food dominated the lives of the woodland people. Frequent rainfall and rich fertile soil along the many feeder streams led to long growing seasons and bountiful harvests in the Lake Erie Basin. During the warm months, women cleared fields using slash-and-burn techniques, then planted crops of corn,

---

[24] Vietzen, Indians of the Lake Erie Basin, or Lost Nations, 64.

beans, potatoes, and squash in the rich black soil there, and natives began growing corn in the eastern United States as early as two thousand years ago.[25] Families dug six-feet deep circular storage pits in their homes to store food for winter use. Storage pits were lined with bark on the sides and stone in the bottom. Leaves were used between layers of produce to prevent freezing. Corn was usually roasted, boiled, dried, and ground. Erie cooks used mortars and pestles made of stone or wood to grind corn into meal, and made a mush out of corn meal, dried fruit, and water. Some villages had large community grindstones made of granite or sandstone that multiple families shared. Pumpkins and squash were cleaned and cut into noodle-like strips, then dried beside a fire. Once dry, the strips were put into pouches which were hung from roof poles inside the longhouse. They could then be boiled until soft for a satisfying winter meal.[26]

The immense forests along the lake were plentiful sources of food for the Erie as well. Women and children gathered wild fruits and berries, including raspberries, blackberries, strawberries, apples, grapes, plums, and cherries. Many of these were dried and saved for the colder months as well. Several varieties of nuts grew wild for gathering, including acorns, walnuts, chestnuts,

---

[25] Vietzen, Indians of the Lake Erie Basin, or Lost Nations, 22.
[26] Vietzen, Indians of the Lake Erie Basin, or Lost Nations, page 154.

hazelnuts, and beechnuts.[27] Women also tapped the abundant maple trees to make syrup.

Erie men hunted bear, deer, elk, raccoon, beaver, rabbit, and several varieties of wild rodents and fowl with bows and arrows or small, lightweight axes made of stone. Deer were the most important animal to the Erie. According to Lupold, to feed a village of about one hundred people, at least four deer needed to be killed per day, which wasn't always possible. As a result, malnutrition was common.[28] Some animals that were killed were eaten right away, but the rest were smoked and dried for future consumption. Women did all of the meat and hide processing. Large pieces of meat were cut into small strips, laid out on slabs of wood or bark, and placed around a fire to be smoked. All dried meat and other foodstuffs were hung from roof poles and posts inside the longhouses where wild animals could not access them until they were needed.[29]

The Erie used deer for much more than food; almost every part was utilized in some way. They made tool handles and arrow points from antlers. Hoofs were boiled and made into glue. Tough sinews were used for thread, bowstrings, and snares. Bones were used to create many different tools, including awls, hooks, harpoons, needles, combs, digging hoes, and skin-dressing tools, as well as

[27] Lupold, The Forgotten People: The Woodland Erie, 31.
[28] Vietzen, Indians of the Lake Erie Basin, or Lost Nations, page 151.
[29] Vietzen, Indians of the Lake Erie Basin, or Lost Nations, page 154.

handles for other tools and ornaments. Bags and containers were made from stomachs and bladders. Hides were important for moccasins, clothing and shelter, and curing and processing them took up a great deal of time.[30]

After skinning an animal such as a deer, the women stretched the skin over the ground or a frame made of tree branches; they scraped the hide with sharp rocks or bone to remove the fat and flesh and left the hide to dry. Sometimes, they left the hair on for winter clothing or

blankets. This was especially true of thick bear skins, which provided a warm covering from the bitter cold. Other times, the hair was scraped off or removed by soaking the hide in lye made from ashes and water. Once dry, the skins were smoked over open fires, soaked in water for a day or two, then wrung out and dried by a fire. The hides were slowly smoked a second time and worked constantly to keep them from becoming stiff. To make the hides especially soft and well-preserved, the Eries would soak oak bark in water to produce tannic acid and then soak the hides in this mixture for a few days until it was ready to be dried again and used.[31] Once cured, the hides were used to make clothing, moccasins, bags, pouches, and more.

[30] Lupold, The Forgotten People: The Woodland Erie, 32.
[31] Vietzen, Indians of the Lake Erie Basin, or Lost Nations, 152.

Since they lived near water, fish and shellfish were also a large part of the Erie diet. Men fished for bass, pickerel and other fish with hooks and nets weighted by stone, and women dug for oysters and clams. Sandusky Bay, on the southwestern side of Lake Erie, was an especially common fishing site. The Erie and other Iroquois tribes found that certain tree barks produced ichthyotoxins when crushed and placed in small pools of water, which paralyzed fish and made it easy to catch them in great quantities with nets. Women and children usually fished in this manner. Judging by the large number of fish skeletons, scales, and shells found in refuse pits, archeologists believe that the Erie diet included a lot of fish, especially when hunting was unsuccessful. Erie women made a soup out of boiled fish and mussels.[32] Surplus fish were also smoked and dried for later consumption. Fish were scaled and split into flat fillets which were laid on slabs of wood or bark and placed around fires where they could be cured by smoke.[33]

To create tools and weapons, the Erie, like other Iroquois tribes, used celts, a piece of antler, stone, or metal with a broken, shaved, or ground-down beveled edge that could cut through flesh or animal hide. Several flint quarries in the Lake Erie Basin made it easy to access the stone for the Erie and neighboring tribes. They used flint to make

---

[32] Vietzen, Indians of the Lake Erie Basin, or Lost Nations, 22.
[33] Vietzen, Indians of the Lake Erie Basin, or Lost Nations, 153.

arrow points and spearheads for hunting, fishing, and fighting, as well as knives for cutting meat, hides, bark and plants, and small axes and chisels for chopping wood for fires and building materials. According to Vietzen, flint was just as vital to the Eries' existence as deer, corn, or trees.[34]

Winters were difficult in the Lake Erie Basin, especially with bitterly cold winds blowing off the water, but the natives learned to use the deep snows to their advantage. Snow drifts insulated the longhouses, making them warmer and less drafty and a coating of snow over food storage pits protected the corn, squash, and pumpkins inside from freezing or spoiling. Deep snows slowed game such as rabbits, elk, and deer, making them easier prey for hunters on snowshoes. When a large animal such as a bear or elk was killed, the Erie made toboggans out of tree branches and deer hide to transport the carcasses back to camp.

A vast network of trails wound through the forests, upon which various tribes and wild game traveled back and forth between villages and hunting grounds. These often became routes upon which modern roads and highways were eventually built. Portage trails between the Cuyahoga and Muskingum Rivers were important, as was the Lake Trail, which followed the southern shore of Lake

---

[34] Vietzen Indians of the Lake Erie Basin, or Lost Nations, 237.

Erie from present-day Buffalo, New York to Toledo, Ohio.

Eries followed the Iroquois political structure, which consisted of a tribe of united familial clans, which took their name from various animals, including wolf, turtle, bear, elk, wildcat, and raccoon, and used a heraldic insignia called a totem to represent themselves.[35] Clans were organized matrilineally, meaning inheritance came from one's mother, and each family was led by a matron, while eight male chiefs usually led the entire tribe. Individuals always married exogenously, or outside of their clan. Upon marriage, the husband moved into the wife's family home, and, if he proved to be a poor husband, he could be thrown out at any time.[36]

Women held positions of great importance in tribal councils and participated in decision-making equally with male leaders.[37] According to local legend, Queen Yagowanea was the most revered leader of the Erie. Because her reputation for fairness was known everywhere, she was often called upon to mediate during disputes between other tribes. She insisted upon a policy of neutrality in interactions with the Iroquois in the east and the Hurons in the west. Though they were known for neutrality, the Erie were not a meek tribe. In fact, the Erie

[35] Kimm, The Iroquois: A History of the Six Nations of New York, 194.
[36] Kimm, The Iroquois: A History of the Six Nations of New York, 246.
[37] Lupold, The Forgotten People: The Woodland Erie, 17.

warriors were known and feared, and they gave power to the Queen's policy of armed neutrality by intimidating other tribes into leaving them alone, for the most part.[38]

Individuals derived economic security through loyalty to his or her clan and tribe. Like most Native American peoples, the Erie had no concept of private land ownership. All land was tribal land, occupied and used by individual clans and bands. Tribes were territorial, however. It was not uncommon for one tribe to invade another and push them out of valuable territory, as the Iroquois did to the Erie in the 1650s.

The Erie judicial system was led by the clan elders or chiefs, but there were no formal laws or codes. Those guilty of murder were put to death by a member of the victim's family and then buried with their victims after some part of their anatomy was removed and placed at the victim's head. Treason was also a capital offense. Anyone who revealed tribal secrets or military plans to the enemy was burned alive.[39]

Erie religion, like that of other Iroquois tribes, centered on the belief in a "Great Spirit," which they called Manitou, who created the world and helped his people to understand the mysteries of the earth and solve their problems, with a large number of lesser spirits beneath it.

---

[38] Spencer, Erie, A History, 16.
[39] Vietzen, Indians of the Lake Erie Basin, or Lost Nations, 157.

According to Iroquois legend, the Great Spirit lived in the heavens and created humans out of red earth.[40] A shaman, or priest-doctor, was one of the most important leaders of the tribe because he was responsible for curing the sick and communicating with the spirits. According to one legend, the Erie were the Great Spirit's "favorite children," so he gave them the land along the "great unsalted sea," and told them the "hills and plains abound in game to feed you and clothe you; the pure water from the streams will slake your thirst; the fields will yield a hundred fold returns from (your) labors…the lake will furnish you fish in abundance…health-giving breezes…will strengthen your sons and daughters in mind and body so that you…may be the pride of your race."[41]

Like all Native Americans, the Eries used plants to create medicines, poultices, and potions. One common treatment was called the Black Drink Medicine, which was used in a ceremony for purity of body and soul. Made of button snakeroot, wild tobacco flowers, spicewood, cedar, various berries, grapevine, mistletoe, horsemint, and oak brewed together as a tea and served in conch shell cups, it induced violent vomiting thought to rid the patient of whatever malady that ailed him.[42] Medicine and religion were not separated in the minds of the Erie, and

[40] Moulthrop, Samuel P., Iroquois, Ernest Hart, Rochester, New York: Earnest Hart, 1901), 5.
[41] Spencer, Herbert, Erie, A History, (published by the author, 1962), 10.
[42] Vietzen, Indians of the Lake Erie Basin, or Lost Nations, 171.

both were related to the spirit and the breath. Thus, pipe smoking was considered sacred and significant, and sometimes healing.

Tobacco grew wild in eastern North America at this time, so smoking was common among most native tribes. This was an important custom because the mysterious rise and vanishing of the smoke led the people to believe that the breath of the smoker ascended to the Great Spirit through the smoke, carrying his prayers along with it. For the Erie, like other Iroquois tribes, smoking during a council or ceremony was a kind of burnt offering or animated prayer to the Great Spirit. Elbow-shaped pipes were usually made of clay with round bowls at the base. Sometimes, a hollow stem or reed was attached with clay to a bowl made of carved slate, pipestone, calcium-calcite, or sandstone and effigies of important animals, usually birds, were carved on pipes to give them higher significance.

For important religious ceremonies, the Erie made huge altar pipes, which could be ten to twenty times bigger than personal pipes. They featured a large, flat base that sat on the altar instead of being held or passed around. These were usually made of sandstone and carved with larger animals, such as wolves, turtles, fish, and even human forms.[43]

---

[43] Vietzen, Indians of the Lake Erie Basin, or Lost Nations, 205.

In addition to pure tobacco leaves, the Erie smoked a concoction known as kinnikinnick, meaning "that which is mixed." This mixture of red willow bark, dogwood leaves, dried berries sumac, Yerba Santa, and other plants, as well as tobacco, was very common and important for most Iroquois tribes.[44] Dried sumac leaves were also smoked often and because of the pleasant odor emitted when burned, sumac was also used for dyeing, tanning and incense. Smoking was considered beneficial for both mind and body and some mixtures produced drowsiness or pain relief for the sick or wounded.[45]

The Erie, like other Iroquois tribes, worshipped the sun and moon as well as the Great Spirit. After a harsh winter of snow storms and cold winds, the natives would give thanks for the return of the sun in the early spring. The moon was also idolized as it was the "sun" of the night sky.[46] All Iroquois tribes followed the lunar year, with thirteen moons of 28 days each, counting from one visible phase to the next.[47]

Rituals and feasts were important to the Erie as a way of showing gratitude to a generous God, celebrating success, and mourning the dead. They gave burnt offerings to the spirits on an altar before all important events. Prized

---

[44] Nozedar, Adele, The Element Encyclopedia of Native Americans, (Harper Element), 298.
[45] Vietzen, Indians of the Lake Erie Basin, or Lost Nations, 203.
[46] Vietzen, Indians of the Lake Erie Basin, or Lost Nations, 173.
[47] Kimm, The Iroquois: A History of the Six Nations of New York, 420.

materials, often tobacco, were placed into a small package, which was then placed on the altar and the shaman applied a fire brand to the package. If the offering lit on fire immediately and was consumed by the flames, it signified that the Great Spirit accepted the offering and gave his blessing, a good omen. If not, reconsiderations might be made. When famine, drought, or plagues struck, the tribe gave larger offerings to the Great Spirit. Leaders dug pits and lit fires inside them, into which tribe members threw favorite objects, prized ornaments, weapons, and anything they believed would be significant enough to appease the Great Spirit so he would come to their aid. During drastic times, a human sacrifice would be made. A young warrior was chosen and given the best of everything for his pleasure during his last days on earth, including beautiful maidens.[48]

Marriage was another sacred ceremony for the Eries, and vows were entered into solemnly and earnestly. The chief or shaman slit the wrists of the bride and groom and bound them together with a string of beads so that their blood flowed together and intermixed, symbolizing the two lives becoming one.[49] Widows and widowers waited a full year before considering a new spouse, when a feast was given to celebrate the choosing of a new mate.

[48] Vietzen, Indians of the Lake Erie Basin, or Lost Nations, 171.
[49] Vietzen, Indians of the Lake Erie Basin, or Lost Nations, 156.

Adultery and infidelity were serious crimes, punished by torture and death followed by a disgraceful burial.

Much of the Erie existence centered on agriculture, and the Green Corn Dance was an important annual occurrence. This yearly festival giving thanks for the corn, rain, sun, and good harvest was held at the time the new crop of corn was ready to eat. Before consuming any of the new corn, the Great Spirit must be properly thanked during this festival. Medicine men led the ceremony by choosing the finest ears of corn, which were then cooked in a large pot, and placed on a rack of sticks over a fire as a sacrifice to the Great Spirit. The shamans sang and danced around the offertory fire until the corn was completely burned to ashes. Dancers carried green corn stalks and chanted while dancing. After the sacrificial corn burned to ash, a new fire was kindled on the same spot and women prepared a great feast for everyone, including corn from the new harvest and many other foods, which lasted for days.[50]

Every ten years, a Feast of the Dead took place, during which the Erie removed remains of loved ones from their platforms or graves and scraped the remaining flesh from the bones, which were then wrapped in skins and taken to a pit where final burial was made. Several days of feasting, dancing, and rituals took place as the shaman

---

[50] Vietzen, Indians of the Lake Erie Basin, or Lost Nations, 172.

lowered the bones into the pit along with offerings of beads, pendants, and other treasured items.[51]

The Erie considered several animals sacred, but especially birds, because they were believed to be messengers of the Great Spirit. The eagle, for example, flies so high in the sky that they seem to disappear from sight, so the natives assumed they must fly to another world where the Great Spirit lives, directing the sun and rain. Because of this reverence for birds, the Erie and other Iroquois used feathers on arrow shafts to help them fly quickly and directly to their destination.[52] They also used feathers for adornments on clothing or headdresses.

While there are no living descendants of the Erie to speak for them, their graves can tell their stories. Several details of Erie society have been learned by studying how they buried their dead. Using digging tools made of sticks or the shoulder blades of deer or elk, the Erie buried their deceased in burial mounds, in rectangular graves between 24 and 48 inches deep, or, sometimes, in mass burial pits. Most cemeteries were found on hillsides and cremation was not common. Interestingly, archeologists have found red and yellow stains on the bones of many skeletons where the bodies were painted with ochre, usually on the head and in the reproductive regions to help keep them

<hr>

[51] Vietzen, Indians of the Lake Erie Basin, or Lost Nations, 172.
[52] Vietzen, Indians of the Lake Erie Basin, or Lost Nations, 171.

Like burial sites, refuse pits often tell a great deal about native peoples as well. These cistern-like pits were usually three to four feet in diameter and four to six feet deep although some as large as thirty feet in diameter have been found.[61] Bark lined the sides, and stones lay along the bottom.[62] Refuse, such as broken pottery, fish skeletons and scales, mussel shells, antlers, and animal bones, was thrown into these pits and later covered with ashes and clean earth. Evidence of trade with Europeans has also been found in these pits, including glass beads and arrow points made from European brass. Once everything from a food storage pit was consumed, it usually became a refuse pit. Many human bones have also been found in these pits, suggesting that they were also used as burial pits for unimportant or unfortunate people, perhaps criminals or captives.

Thousands of fragments called potsherds prove that the Erie were extensive pottery makers who utilized a high degree of skill in their designs and decorations. They made elongated jars with everted rims, spherical bodies, and round bases, as well as pitchers, which were basically jars with pointed noses on one side of the rim. Pottery was made from naturally occurring clay found locally and tempered with finely pounded grit or shell to make it more

---

[61] Houghton, "The Characteristics of Iroquoian Village Sites of Western New York," 511.
[62] Vietzen, Indians of the Lake Erie Basin, or Lost Nations, 161.

durable and less likely to crack. Coiling was the most common method of making pottery, which involved rolling the clay into long, thin snakes and then building a pot by coiling the snakes round and round on top of each other to make the outer walls of a bowl or pot. The layers were smoothed by hand once all the coils were put in place. The vessels were placed outside to dry in the sun and then heated in a fire to harden them and make sure all moisture was removed. Colors ranged from reddish-tan to black, with darker colors usually resulting from repeated use as cooking vessels over a smoky open fire.[63]

Few potsherds have been found on Erie sites that do not have some form of decoration or pattern. The Erie used two methods of decoration for their pottery: incision and impression. Incision involved using a sharp object to carve or draw designs into the clay while it was still soft, and usually involved linear patterns such as chevron, herringbone, cross-hatches or parallel lines. Some pottery was brush-marked with a bundle of reeds or twigs while still soft to produce a series of parallel marks. Impression, on the other hand, involved pressing cylindrical, triangular, square, or oblong-shaped objects into the soft clay to form intricate patterns and designs. Many objects were used to make impressions in pottery, including rough

---

[63] Vietzen, Indians of the Lake Erie Basin, or Lost Nations, 161.

sections of antlers or tree bark. These created a texture in the clay, giving it a more secure grip for carrying.[64]

In addition to creating artistic pottery, women decorated clothing, wampum belts and other possessions with red, blue or yellow ink made from the leaves and blossoms of plants, such as sumac, as well as berries. These plant parts were ground in mortars with stone or wooden pestles and mixed with water to create paint or dye. These primitive artists used porcupine quills as pens.[65]

In their little free time when not farming, hunting, building shelter, preparing food, making goods and tools, or fighting, the Erie enjoyed sports, such as target shooting, hockey, and wrestling. Friendly gambling was common among the men. Lacrosse was highly strenuous and competitive, and games could go on for days. The Erie also enjoyed a game in which several peach or plum pits were placed in a bowl and players competed to see who could make the most bounce out when the bowl was slammed on the ground. Score was kept with intricately carved counting sticks. Another game, called snow snake, was played during the winter. In a competition similar to javelin, a five-foot long wooden snake was carved out of hard wood, such as hickory, and players took turns hurling the snake down an icy course to see who could throw it

[64] Vietzen, Indians of the Lake Erie Basin, or Lost Nations, 187-188.
[65] Kimm, The Iroquois: A History of the Six Nations of New York, 260.

the farthest. A type of theater-like storytelling was also popular during feasts and festivals.[66]

European Contact

According to Lupold, there were at least 20,000 Iroquois in the area that is now the northeastern United States when Christopher Columbus first stepped foot in the Americas in 1492.[67] The Erie occupied the southern shore of Lake Erie from 1300-1655 and for most of the sixteenth century, various tribes continually made war with each other, as each small tribe functioned for itself. Raiding the villages of nearby tribes was common amongst the Iroquois and they used warfare to obtain goods, tools, furs, and captives, as well as to push others out of valuable territory.

Around 1570, five Iroquois tribes in present-day New York State, the Seneca, Cayuga, Onondaga, Oneida, and Mohawk, organized an alliance to provide a stronger defense against attacks from Algonquian tribes in the north. Mohawk Chief Hiawatha, a passionate and convincing orator, and Deganawida, a spiritual leader known as The Great Peacemaker, initiated the confederacy, which they called Haudenosaunee. The goal of the Iroquois League, or League of Peace and Power, was to establish a universal peace among the Iroquois

---

[66] Vietzen, Indians of the Lake Erie Basin, or Lost Nations, 157-158.
[67] Lupold, The Forgotten People: The Woodland Erie, 13.

people, even though each tribe maintained its independence and identity. Fifty leaders from the five tribes met for three days on the banks of the Onondaga Lake[68] and agreed that all tribes would come to the aid of any member tribe who was attacked. In effect, moving against one League tribe meant declaring war on all of them. The exact historical details of this union are hazy and surrounded in mythology, but historians agree that the first people to join were the Mohawk and Oneida, followed by the Onondaga, Cayuga, and Seneca.[69] According to legend, Hiawatha's wife and children were killed by another tribe, but he chose peace instead of revenge, and encouraged other tribes to do the same by establishing an agreement that united the tribes together.[70] The Iroquois League called their agreement The Tree of Peace or the Great Law of Peace, and it was much like a constitution, although they had no written language. Instead, the law was conveyed by symbols displayed on wampum belts as well as an oral tradition. The ideas of the Great Law of Peace influenced those who authored the United States Constitution, as acknowledged by the U.S. Congress in 1988.[71] The Tuscarora Tribe joined the league sometime in the early eighteenth century. Four tribes, the

---

[68] Kimm, S.C. The Iroquois: A History of the Six Nations of New York. (Middleburgh, New York: Press of Pierre W. Danforth, 1900), 103.
[69] Nozedar, The Element Encyclopedia of Native Americans, 241.
[70] Ditchfield, Christin, Northeast Indians, (Chicago: Heinemann Library, 2012), 11.
[71] Nozedar, The Element Encyclopedia of Native Americans, 220.

Erie, Huron, Susquehanna, and Neutrals, did not join the confederacy. This would prove a disastrous mistake.

In 1534, French explorer Jacques Cartier crossed the Atlantic Ocean and sailed up the St. Lawrence River to present-day Montreal, taking possession of the surrounding land for King Francis I and calling it New France. Because of political unrest at home and wars with England and Spain, however, the French government did little to expand colonization in the New World. In 1603, French explorer Samuel de Champlain led an expedition to Quebec and made a permanent settlement there, founding the colony of Canada. From here, explorers and fur traders soon made their way down Lake Ontario and Lake Erie. By the mid-seventeenth century, French explorers, fur traders, and missionaries began entering Native territory south of the Great Lakes. They called the Erie people *Nation du Chat,* Cat Nation, because they wore beautiful robes made of the skins of the wild panthers, pumas, and lynx that commonly roamed the region, using the tails to create borders and adornments.[72] *Erie* in the Iroquois language means long tail, referencing the panther, who uses its long tail to balance high in the tree limbs.

In 1609, Henry Hudson, an English navigator working for the Dutch, discovered the river that would bear his

---

[72] Lupold, The Forgotten People: The Woodland Erie 25.

name in present-day New York State and claimed the land up to what is now Albany, New York for the Dutch. In 1620, the first English settlers reached North America at Plymouth, Massachusetts and claimed the land for the British. There were now three European nations competing for land and resources, especially furs, on Iroquois land. This put a strain on the Native Americans who had always hunted these animals, leading to competition for resources. As the tribes of the Iroquois League became more dependent on European goods, they sought to expand their territory in order to control the fur trade, which meant eliminating their neighbors, the Hurons, Neutrals, and Eries.

Archeological evidence proves that the Erie traded with Europeans or with other tribes who had obtained European goods, but there is no written record of direct contact between Europeans and the Cat Nation. Excavations of Erie villages have uncovered pieces of flintlock guns, metal knife blades, iron nails, and pieces of stoneware from the early seventeenth century. However, as the Europeans were more concentrated in the East, the Eries did not obtain as many muskets, knives or iron axes as their Iroquois cousins, leaving them at a disadvantage in tribal warfare. After the European arrival, some steel tools were used, but most of the Erie continued to use the same bone or stone implements they always had.

Intertribal trade was more common; various tribes traded extensively with each other for obsidian, copper, flint, salt, pipestone, and tobacco.[73]

The first written record of the Erie came in 1624 from Father Gabriel Sagard, who was working with the Hurons and made a dictionary of their language in 1639.[74] Jesuit missionaries first recorded the presence of the Cat Nation south of Lake Erie in 1635. The Jesuits attempted missions among the New York Iroquois, but never established any mission among the Erie, and, quite possibly, never had direct contact with them at all.[75] They had very little luck with the Iroquois, because of their hostile ways, but historians have learned a great deal about these cultures from the secondary accounts recorded by the Jesuits.

Warfare

For centuries, the Iroquois had raided each other often, for revenge, glory, territory, loot, or captives. Lupold describes the Iroquois as adept diplomats, but they were also aggressive warriors who attacked enemies fiercely and were cruel to those they conquered. They considered themselves at war with all native tribes who were not members of the Iroquois League, as well as European

---

[73] Lupold, The Forgotten People: The Woodland Erie, 10.
[74] "Erie Indians," Case Western Reserve University. Accessed 15 August 2020, https://case.edu/ech/articles/e/erie-indians.
[75] Lupold, The Forgotten People: The Woodland Erie, 23.

settlers and soldiers who tried to infiltrate their territory. Their method of warfare involved "sneaking up on the enemy like foxes, fighting like lions, and disappearing into the woods like birds."[76] Their war strategy favored extermination and adoption rather than conquest, and their territory would likely have extended over most of North America if it had not been for the arrival and interference of Europeans. Their domain stretched from the St. Lawrence River in the north to the Blue Ridge Mountains in the south, and from the Hudson in the east to the Mississippi in the west. Unfortunately for the Eries, their homeland was smack in the middle of this huge swath of coveted terrain.

The Eries tried to maintain their policy of neutrality, but they did not hesitate to retaliate when attacked or treated with injustice. War was considered an opportunity for fortune and glory by most Native Americans. Successful warriors were honored and esteemed, and death was considered a necessary risk.[77]

Most of what is known about Erie war practices has been gleaned from burial sites of the tribes they fought with, namely bone wounds in skeletal remains. The Cat Nation rarely used firearms, and they made a specific type of arrowhead, which did not feature a notch used to attach

---

[76] Lupold, The Forgotten People: The Woodland Erie, 14.
[77] Spencer, Erie, A History, 17.

the arrow point to the shaft, as many tribes' arrow points did. Erie arrow points, made of antler or flint, were usually about an inch long, triangular, thin, keen-edged, and "frequently beautifully made."[78] These arrowheads, which have been found embedded in the spinal columns and other bones of other tribespeople, reveal how the Erie conducted warfare.[79]

War parties consisted of small contingents of male warriors led by a chief. Raids amongst enemy villages usually took place in the spring or summer, as efforts were focused on hunting and mere survival during the harsh winters. There was no overall commander or rules of warfare. Once the attack began, warriors acted freely according to their own desires. War parties moved through the forests in single-file formations and camped at night. They carried bows and skin quivers with about fifteen arrows tipped with flint or antler. Erie warriors usually used antler arrow points, which were more accurate than flint. These were shaped like bullets, cylindrical with a point at the end, and made by cutting off antler tines and then drilling holes in the wooden arrow shafts to make sockets to hold the points.[80] Tomahawks also dangled from warriors' belts.

---

[78] Houghton, "The Characteristics of Iroquoian Village Sites of Western New York," 512.
[79] Vietzen, Indians of the Lake Erie Basin, or Lost Nations, 83.
[80] Vietzen, Indians of the Lake Erie Basin, or Lost Nations, 160.

Enemies not killed in battle were usually taken as captives to be tortured until they died or adopted into the tribe to replace their own losses. The Iroquois were notorious for torturing their male captives most brutally, so those attacked by the Iroquois would often choose death over capture. According to Lupold, torture might include burning body parts with brands, embers, and hot metal, mutilating the ears, nose, lips, eyes, tongue, and other body parts, tearing out nails, twisting off fingers and driving skewers into finger stumps, pulling sinews out of arms, and, of course, scalping alive. After death, a tortured person's body was usually cooked and eaten.[81] They believed that consuming the body of the captured enemy eliminated his soul and prevented it from traveling to the afterlife.

Other captives, namely children and sometimes women, would be adopted into a tribe to replace those lost to disease or warfare. The new family member would assume the identity of the deceased one and be treated as a normal member of the victorious tribe. Attempts to reclaim captured family members were often a cause of war, as well.

By the beginning of the seventeenth century, the territory of various Iroquois groups was firmly established. The five tribes that made up the Iroquois League, the Mohawk,

---

[81] Lupold, The Forgotten People: The Woodland Erie, 15-16.

Seneca, Cayuga, Onondaga, and Oneida, lived in central and northern New York State. Another tribe which maintained neutrality in wars between the Iroquois and other nations, called the Neutral or Neuter Nation, lived along the Niagara River and the east end of Lake Erie. The Hurons lived north of Lake Erie, and the Tobacco Nation resided south of Lake Huron. The independent Erie people had the entire south shore of Lake Erie, including almost all of present-day Ohio, northwestern Pennsylvania, and some of western New York, to themselves. They controlled the Cuyahoga River Valley, including an important portage path from the Tuscarawas River to the Ohio River.[82]

By 1630, the Erie were moving eastward to escape attacks by western Algonquian-speaking tribes who wanted their territory, but it was war with fellow Iroquois that proved most disastrous for the Cat Nation, a strong warlike people. Despite being basically surrounded by them, they were not intimidated by the reputation or power of the Iroquois League.[83] The Dutch settlers called them *Satanas*, or devils. The principal enemy of the Erie was the Seneca, their neighbors to the north and east, and "the fiercest and most cruel of the Iroquois."[84] The Eries' main strategy was to sustain the initial first attack of their

[82] Lupold, The Forgotten People: The Woodland Erie, 32.
[83] Lupold, The Forgotten People: The Woodland Erie, 33.
[84] Vietzen, Indians of the Lake Erie Basin, or Lost Nations, 24.

rivals, who were armed with European muskets, and then charge on them, firing up to ten poisoned arrows before the Iroquois could reload their guns.

Up to now, the Erie had maintained a position of strict neutrality when members of the Iroquois League were at war, and for this reason, people of other warring tribes often sought refuge in their villages. In 1634, a member of the Mississauga tribe, a branch of the Algonquians, was murdered, and the killer had escaped and taken refuge among the Erie. When the victim's family came to Queen Yagowanea and asked her to turn over the murderer to them for punishment, she agreed. Seneca chiefs who heard of this felt it was a breach of Erie neutrality policy, as Queen Yagowanea appeared to be helping their enemy, the Algonquians. They took this supposed breach as an opportunity to wage war on the Erie. A horrific battle ensued, and about six hundred warriors were killed between both sides before a truce was called and both tribes withdrew.[85] A peace treaty was initiated that lasted for the next twenty years.

In the 1640s, the powerful Iroquois League set upon the destruction of their historic rivals, the Huron, also known as the Wyandot, who lived from present-day Toronto, Canada into Wisconsin. The Hurons were one of the earliest tribes to initiate contact with Europeans. Early in

---

[85] Spencer, Erie, A History, 17.

the seventeenth century, the French established a trading alliance with the Huron and the Algonquians, bitter enemies of the Iroquois League. In 1609, Huron and Algonquian warriors, armed with French muskets, easily defeated the Mohawks, a member of the Iroquois League.[86] From this point forward, the Iroquois League held a grudge against both the Huron and the French, who had supplied them with deadly firepower. The Iroquois soon increased trading with the British and Dutch for modern weapons. For the next thirty years, attacks by both sides were common.

In 1639, the Huron captured over one hundred Iroquois and burned them alive. Ten years later, Seneca and Mohawk war parties attacked Huron villages and killed or captured up to ten thousand. Smallpox and other European diseases devastated the Huron population in the first decades of the seventeenth century, making it much more difficult to defend against attacks. In 1648, fifteen Huron villages were abandoned in one week, and those who were able to escape fled to the Cat Nation for sanctuary.[87] The Erie agreed to help their neighbors, but this invited the wrath of the Iroquois League, especially their old enemies, the Seneca. The Iroquois demanded that the Erie hand over the Huron refugees, but they refused.

---

[86] Lupold, The Forgotten People: The Woodland Erie, 42.
[87] Vietzen, Indians of the Lake Erie Basin, or Lost Nations, 117.

Unfortunately, their generosity would lead to their downfall, because while the Huron were allied with the French, other Iroquois tribes traded mostly with the Dutch and English. Dutch guns gave the Iroquois, especially the Seneca, their reputation for warlike ferocity.[88] Over time, the Iroquois League had become dependent on European goods such as weapons, knives, kettles, and blankets, which they obtained by trading furs, so they sought control of the fur trade, which meant they must eliminate competitors through subjugation or annihilation. By 1640, they had exhausted the beaver supply in their own territory, and needed to branch out.[89] They began by defeating the Tobacco People in 1649, then moved to the Erie, and the Hurons who had gone to live with them, in 1653. The Cat Nation blocked Iroquois access to the fertile hunting grounds of the Ohio River Valley. The Seneca, the Eries' neighbor to the immediate east, were the most populous of the Iroquois member nations and were the first to defend any member of the Iroquois League under threat.[90]

The Erie and Seneca had an existing peace treaty, which was to be renewed in 1653. Thirty Erie ambassadors traveled to the Seneca capital of Sonontouan, in western New York, to negotiate the treaty.[91] During discussions, a

---

88 Nozedar, The Element Encyclopedia of Native Americans, 525.
89 Lupold, The Forgotten People: The Woodland Erie, page 47.
90 "Birth of a Nation," Seneca Nation of Indians, accessed 15 August 2020, https://sni.org/culture/birth-of-a-nation/.

Seneca representative was killed, either by accident or during a heated disagreement, and they retaliated by killing all but five of the Erie ambassadors. This unfortunate episode triggered a string of reprisals that led to all-out war between the Eries and the Iroquois League, allies of the Seneca.

Some accounts describe an athletic competition gone awry as the impetus for war between the Iroquois and Erie. This began with a huge ball game, probably lacrosse, which took place near present-day Buffalo, New York. One hundred men played on each side, with the winners receiving a heavy amount of furs and wampum, shell beads strung together that the natives used as currency. The Iroquois trounced the Cats, so the defeated tribe suggested a foot race to redeem themselves, which they also lost. The embarrassed Erie chief then proposed a wrestling match, but the Iroquois defeated several of the Erie braves. The chief was so angry that he killed his losing warriors himself.[92] Humiliated, the Cat warriors sought revenge militarily instead, and planned a surprise attack on their enemies. The Iroquois were tipped off, however, by a Seneca woman whom they had captured years earlier and lived with them ever since. She snuck away from the Erie camp at night and canoed to her old

[91] Hodge, "Erie Tribe," The Handbook of American Indians North of Mexico. (Washington, D.C.: Smithsonian Institution, 1907), 617.
[92] Becker, Sophie, Sketches of Early Buffalo and the Niagara Region, Buffalo, New York, 1904, 28.

Seneca village, where she warned them of an impending attack. The Iroquois gathered five thousand warriors and met the Eries near the Genesee River.[93] Hand-to-hand conflict ensued, and the Erie, though badly outnumbered, did not retreat, surrender, or ask for quarter.[94] Those who tried to flee were pursued and killed.

There is no written record of this account, only an oral tradition, so it can neither be proven nor refuted, but it does suggest the doggedness of the Erie in the face of their more powerful rivals, and their refusal to back down or give up. This perseverance, while admirable, turned out to be catastrophic. It eventually led to the complete annihilation of their culture. Other sources place this same account between the Kah-Kwahs and Senecas, specifically, which are merely different branches of the same two trees, but the story is much the same.[95]

Whatever the impetus, the Erie soon retaliated, attacking and burning a Seneca town near present-day Buffalo, and ambushing a war party, killing eighty Iroquois warriors. The Jesuits had established a mission with the Onondagas in 1653, and most of what we know about the war between the Erie and Iroquois comes from writings by Jesuit priests. The following year, the Eries captured and

93 Johnson, Crisfield, Centennial History of Erie County, New York, (Buffalo: Printing House of Matthews & Warren, 1876), 27.
94 Becker, Sketches of Early Buffalo and the Niagara Region, 30.
95 Johnson, Elias, Legends, Traditions, and Laws of the Iroquois, or Six Nations and History of the Tuscarora Indians, (Lockport, New York: Union Printing and Publishing, 1881), 114.

killed a well-known Onondaga chief named Annenraes.[96] The Iroquois responded by sending 1,800 warriors in canoes up the Allegheny River and attacking Erie villages there. The Cat Nation, who had about two thousand warriors at the time, retreated to their main village at Riqué. The Iroquois surrounded Riqué and laid siege to the village, where thousands of men, women, and children had holed up inside. Hurling burning wood, the Iroquois set upon the palisaded fort, setting it on fire. The Erie quickly counterattacked with a shower of poisoned arrows, causing many Iroquois casualties. The attackers heaved their canoes over their heads as shields and advanced on the fort. When they reached it, they leaned their canoes upright against the fort wall and used them as scaling ladders to climb up the walls, destroying the Erie defensive barrier which had served them well for decades. With a great number of firearms and ammunition, the Iroquois obliterated the Erie, who mostly had only bows and arrows. Those not killed or captured fled in terror.

The Iroquois suffered a large number of casualties as well, so many that they remained in the area for two months burying their dead and nursing their wounded.[97] Though the Erie did not have the benefit of firearms, as their enemies did, they were strong enough to inflict heavy losses. During this time, a group of three hundred

---

[96] Hodge, "Erie Tribe," 618.
[97] Lupold, The Forgotten People: The Woodland Erie, page 50.

Cat warriors who had gathered in the forest nearby attacked, making several charges across a stream, but the Iroquois beat them back each time, and they ended up retreating into the woods.

For the next four years, Iroquois warriors repeatedly attacked and looted Erie villages. Although the Iroquois had superior weapons and more manpower, the fact that it took them years to defeat the Erie proves the strength of the Cat Nation, unlike the Hurons, who had been defeated in a matter of weeks. The Eries made their last stand in the Cuyahoga River Valley near Copley Swamp in Summit County, Ohio.[98] Of 15,000, just six hundred Erie surrendered to the enemy, the rest were killed, captured, or fled. Those who were slain were burned and buried near West Seneca.[99] Most of the captured were tortured and killed in Iroquois custody, but some women and children were integrated into Iroquois society and lived the remainder of their lives as Iroquois, either as replaced family members or slaves. Young children were often adopted as substitutes for sons or daughters lost by disease or war, and they were raised as Iroquois, so they completely forgot their Erie heritage. Couples or families that were captured together were separated and sent to live in different villages,[100] thereby eliminating the potential

[98] Vietzen, Indians of the Lake Erie Basin, or Lost Nations, page 44.
[99] Becker, Sketches of Early Buffalo and the Niagara Region, 31.
[100] Lupold, The Forgotten People: The Woodland Erie, 52.

for revolt as well as future generations of Erie offspring. One Onondaga war captain named Aharihon boasted of his cruelty to Erie warriors. He claimed to have killed sixty men in battle and burned eighty alive as captives, using small, slow fires to drag out their deaths for hours. He kept count by tattooing a mark on his thigh for each victim.[101]

One especially interesting Erie Village was located on what it is now called Kelleys Island in Lake Erie. This small island could easily be reached by canoe from the mainland near present-day Sandusky or Marblehead, and it was surrounded by earthworks to provide protection. Many Erie tribe members fled to Kelleys Island during the war with the Iroquois. Two petroglyphs, large rock carvings, tell the story of their attempted escape. A huge limestone rock with a smooth, flat surface, 32 feet long, 21 feet wide, and 11 feet high, rises out of the water, upon which the Eries carved symbols and human figures that depict wars, treaties, crimes and turmoils between them and their enemies, as well as the arrival of the Hurons and the final defeat of the vanquished Cat Nation. These messages were interpreted by an Iroquois chief and warrior, and the stone came to be known as Inscription Rock. In 1850, U.S. Army Captain Seth Eastman measured and drew the elements in detail. Though the

---

[101] Lupold, The Forgotten People: The Woodland Erie, 53.

original petroglyphs have been nearly erased by the elements over the centuries, a smaller scale relief was made from Eastman's drawings which can still be seen today at Inscription Rock State Memorial area. Some of the original rock carvings can still be made out, however. On the north side of the island, archeologists found two earthwork forts, villages, and eight mounds with caches of arrows, pipes, bone fishhooks and beads, and potsherds, as well as more petroglyphs cut into a large granite boulder.[102]

In order to have complete control of the fur trade, the Iroquois went on to eliminate the Neutrals in 1656, and finally the Susquehannas in the 1670s. The same fate befell smaller Algonquian tribes of the Ohio River Valley as well. For at least 150 years after the Eries' defeat, the Lake Erie Basin was used by roving groups of European and American Indian fur traders, hunters, and adventurers, but few made permanent settlements.[103] The Iroquois League, which had a population of less than thirty thousand in 1700, controlled all territory from southeastern Canada to Tennessee and Maine to Minnesota.

For several years after their defeat, the lands of the Cat Nation remained uninhabited, except for hunting and

---

[102] Vietzen, Indians of the Lake Erie Basin, or Lost Nations, 70.
[103] Vietzen, Indians of the Lake Erie Basin, or Lost Nations, 20.

fishing parties that traveled through. Eventually, the Seneca, including many Eries that had been taken captive, returned to occupy the area, especially after they were forced from their homes by American settlers. In 1797, this territory was given to them by the New York State government as the Cattaraugus Reservation.[104] The original reservation included fifty square miles along the southern shore of Lake Erie. In 1802, some of this land was sold to the Holland Land Company, but the remaining 21,000 acres still belongs to the Seneca Nation, and includes a courthouse, orphanage, churches, schools, several businesses, and farmlands.[105]

Some of the Huron and Erie who fled the Iroquois invaders settled temporarily with Algonquians in present-day Wisconsin and they became known as Wyandots. Hostile Sioux tribes pushed them back to the East, however, and they found a home in northern Ohio with the Delaware, Shawnee, and Miami tribes. They joined these groups in fighting with the French against the English in the French and Indian War, then fought the Americans as part of the Miami confederacy in the Battle of Fallen Timbers in 1794. Most joined Tecumseh in his fight against the Americans during the War of 1812.[106]

---

[104] Vietzen, Indians of the Lake Erie Basin, or Lost Nations, 189.
[105] "Cattaraugus Indian Reservation Map and Occupants, 1890," Department of the Interior, Washington, D.C. Government Printing Office, 1894. Accessed 25 August 2020, https://accessgenealogy.com/new-york/cattaraugus-indian-reservation-map-and-occupants-1890.htm.
[106] Lupold, The Forgotten People: The Woodland Erie, 54.

After this, their fate follows the pattern of suffering and relocation endured by all Native American peoples at the hands of the United States government. The Wyandot Tribe was relocated to a reservation in Kansas in 1843,

making them the last Native American tribe to leave Ohio.[107]

Some historians believe that Erie remnants resurfaced on the Upper Ohio River in western Pennsylvania around 1670 under the name Mingo or Mingua, an Algonquian word meaning "rascal." This group later migrated down the Ohio River, joined with the Wyandots and moved westward.[108] Others believe that Erie refugees, along with survivors of the Neutral Tribe, migrated southward to the Carolinas and became known as the Catawbas. As late as 1680, the Iroquois were still bent on the destruction of the Erie, tracking down and killing or capturing a band that was living in the Ohio River Valley in southern Pennsylvania that year.[109] The Iroquois eventually joined a large group of remnants of various Native tribes, including the Erie, Conestoga, Oneida, Cayuga, Mohawk, Tuscarora, Onondaga, and Wyandot, and became known collectively as the Seneca-Cayuga Nation.

---

[107] Nozedar, The Element Encyclopedia of Native Americans, 675.
[108] Lupold, The Forgotten People: The Woodland Erie, 55.
[109] May, John D. "Erie," Oklahoma Historical Society, accessed 17 August 2020, https://www.okhistory.org/publications/enc/entry.php?entry=ER002.

During the American Revolution, the Seneca aligned themselves with the British, and General George Washington sent a battalion of five thousand troops to defeat the tribe. To escape, they relocated to new villages and settlements in western New York, which became reservations. In 1794, the Nations of the Iroquois Confederacy, including many descendants of the now-defunct Erie tribe, signed the Treaty of Canandaigua, one of the earliest peace treaties between Native Americans and the United States government, which guaranteed them land rights in western New York State that are still recognized today. Another treaty three years later ceded more tribal lands to American settlers.[110]

In 1831, this group exchanged 40,000 acres in Ohio for 67,000 acres in Indian Territory, otherwise known as Oklahoma, in a treaty with United States commissioner James B. Gardner. They were initially reluctant to leave, and the journey to Oklahoma took an excruciating eight months, delayed by storms, floods, illness, and death. They traveled on steamboats down the Sandusky River, then over land from Dayton to St. Louis, then to the Cowskin River in Oklahoma. Life on the reservation changed little for the first 25 years. The natives settled on single-family farms or ranches, as opposed to collective villages, where they built log cabins and homemade

---

[110] Nozedar, Adele, The Element Encyclopedia of Native Americans, 526.

furniture. Many learned English and adapted to American ways of life, such as buying goods from merchants rather than making all possessions by hand. There was a blacksmith, miller, tailor, cooper, and a Methodist church on the reservation, but the inhabitants were not interested in a school for their children.[111]

In 1861, while the U.S. was fighting the Civil War, the Seneca and Shawnee signed a treaty with the Confederate States of America, but hundreds of their horses and cattle were commandeered by Union Army forces from Kansas in 1862.[112] Because of this, most of the Seneca-Cayuga and Shawnee people moved to the Ottawa reservation in Kansas, where they remained.

In 1867, an Omnibus Treaty was signed which provided for the sale of the lands of several native tribes, including the Seneca-Cayuga, in Oklahoma. The Seneca were incorporated under the provisions of the Oklahoma Indian Welfare Act of 1936, establishing tribal elections for chief, councilmen, and secretary-treasurer. This law enabled tribes and individual families to obtain financial credit and land, thus encouraging tribal governments to adopt written constitutions and increasing tribal participation in business and government, which led to greater Indian influence in government programs.

---

[111] Wright, Muriel, "Seneca," Seneca-Cayuga Nation, accessed 28 August 2020, http://sctribe.com/history/a-guide-to-the-indian-tribes-of-ok-excerpts/.
[112] Wright, "Seneca."

Conclusion

The populations of virtually all Native American tribes were decimated by the diseases, warfare, and forced relocation that followed European explorers and settlers to their homelands. For the Erie, however, their downfall was caused by the actions of their fellow men. The life of aboriginal peoples was a hard one; only the toughest survived. While the Erie were a doughty, intelligent, and courageous people, their independence brought about their ruin, allowing them to be swallowed up by a larger nation. Their generosity and willingness to shelter those in need invited the wrath of a foe they could not survive against. Luckily, plentiful remains of their society, from pottery to bones to rock carvings, have been unearthed in the forests along Lake Erie, allowing archeologists, anthropologists, and historians to piece together the story of their existence. Experts have also gleaned much about them from their cousins, the Iroquois, but they remain an entity unto themselves, separated from the relatives who destroyed them.

Undoubtedly, some Erie DNA must survive in the descendants of those who were adopted into Iroquois tribes over three centuries ago, but their society as a people, is gone. Fortunately, the crystal waters that bear their name live on, and they are as alive as ever, providing drinking water for over twelve million people in the

United States and Canada as well as a home for a dearth of wildlife. Because it is the shallowest and warmest of the Great Lakes, Lake Erie is also the most biologically productive of the five,[113] making it easy to understand why the Iroquois League coveted this territory.

Though the story of the Cat Nation is a brief one compared to other Native American tribes, it is clearly one worth remembering.

Online Resources

Other Native American history titles by Charles River Editors

Bibliography

Bowne, Eric E. (2005). The Westo Indians: slave traders of the early colonial South. Tuscaloosa, Ala.: University of Alabama Press. ISBN 0-8173-1454-7. OCLC 56214192.

Bowne, Eric E. (2006). "Westo Indians". The New Georgia Encyclopedia. Georgia Humanities Council and the University of Georgia Press.

Engelbrecht, William E. (1991). "Erie". The Bulletin: Journal of the New York State Archaeological Association (102): 2–12. OCLC 17823564.

---

[113] "Lake Erie," United States Environmental Protection Agency, accessed 27 August 2020, https://www.epa.gov/greatlakes/lake-erie.

Engelbrecht, William E.; Lynne P. Sullivan (1996). "Cultural context". In Lynne P. Sullivan (ed.). Reanalyzing the Ripley Site: earthworks and late prehistory on the Lake Erie Plain. New York State Museum Bulletin 489. Albany: University of the State of New York, the State Education Department. pp. 14–27 [volume References, 176–87]. ISBN 1-55557-202-2. OCLC 38565296.

Hewitt, J. N. B. (1907). "Erie". In Frederick Webb Hodge (ed.). Handbook of American Indians north of Mexico, part 1. BAE Bulletin 30. Washington, D.C.: Government Printing Office. pp. 430–32.

Smith, Marvin T. (1987). Archaeology of aboriginal cultural change in the interior Southeast: depopulation during the early historic period. Ripley P. Bullen Monographs in Anthropology and History 6. Gainesville, Fla.: University Press of Florida. OCLC 15017891.

White, Marian E. (1961). Iroquois culture history in the Niagara Frontier area of New York State. University of Michigan Museum of Anthropology Anthropological Papers 16. Ann Arbor, Mich. OCLC 18903624.

White, Marian E. (1971). "Ethnic identification and Iroquois groups in western New York and Ontario". Ethnohistory. 18 (1): 19–38. doi:10.2307/481592. JSTOR 481592.

White, Marian E. (1978). "Erie". In Bruce G. Trigger (ed.). Handbook of North American Indians, Vol. 15: Northeast. Washington, D.C.: Smithsonian Institution. pp. 412–17.

Wright, Roy A. (1974). "The People of the Panther-a long Erie tale (an ethnohistory of the southwestern Iroquoians)". In Michael K. Foster (ed.). Papers in linguistics from the 1972 Conference on Iroquoian Research. Mercury Series Paper 10. Ottawa: National Museum of Man. Ethnology Division. pp. 47–118.

Free Books by Charles River Editors

We have brand new titles available for free most days of the week. To see which of our titles are currently free, click on this link.

Discounted Books by Charles River Editors

We have titles at a discount price of just 99 cents everyday. To see which of our titles are currently 99 cents, click on this link.